PYTHON UNVEILED

A COMPREHENSIVE GUIDE TO MASTERING PYTHON PROGRAMMING

DR ASHOK JAHAGIRDAR | PHD
(INFORMATION TECHNOLOGY)

Made with ♥ on the Notion Press Platform
www.notionpress.com

Contents

Preface

Welcome to "Python Unveiled: Comprehensive Guide to Mastering Python Programming".

It's a roadmap for both beginners and seasoned developers seeking to delve deep into the versatile world of Python programming.

Python has emerged as a cornerstone in the realm of computer science and software development. Its simplicity, readability, and scalability have made it a favorite among programmers, enabling them to create anything from simple scripts to complex applications and frameworks. Its extensive libraries and vast community support have cemented its position as a language of choice for a wide array of industries, from web development and data analysis to artificial intelligence and scientific computing.

This comprehensive guide is meticulously designed to take you on an journey through Python's fundamental concepts, advanced techniques, and practical applications. Whether you're stepping into the coding universe for the first time or looking to enhance your proficiency, this book offers a structured approach to mastering Python's syntax, data structures, object-oriented programming principles, and more.

My aim is to provide a holistic learning experience that combines theoretical foundations with hands-on exercises and real-world examples. Each chapter is thoughtfully crafted to build upon the previous one, ensuring a gradual yet thorough understanding of Python's intricacies. From basic concepts to complex topics.

This book strives to equip you with the tools and knowledge necessary to become a proficient Python developer.

It's important to note that programming is not just about mastering syntax; it's about cultivating problem-solving skills and fostering a mindset of continuous learning and innovation. This book aims not only to teach Python but also to instill in you the confidence to tackle new problems and develop solutions using Python's flexible and powerful features.

One of Python's greatest treasures is its versatility. We'll explore the vast landscape of applications Python serves—from web development with Django and Flask, scientific computing with NumPy and SciPy, to data analysis with Pandas and machine learning with TensorFlow and scikit-learn.

The possibilities are vast.

As you embark on this enriching expedition through "Python Unveiled," I encourage you to embrace curiosity, persistence, and creativity. Allow this book to be your companion in unraveling the mysteries of Python, and may it inspire you to explore the vast possibilities that coding with Python brings.

Happy coding!

Dr. Ashok Jahagirdar

PhD (Information Technology)

January 2024.

CHAPTER ONE

Getting Started with Python

Welcome to the exciting world of Python programming! In this chapter, we'll cover the basics to get you up and running with Python.

Introduction to Python

Python is a high-level, versatile programming language known for its readability and simplicity.

Developed by Guido van Rossum in the late 1980s, Python has gained immense popularity due to its ease of learning and extensive community support.

Its versatility makes it suitable for various applications, from web development and data analysis to artificial intelligence and scientific computing.

Setting Up Python

Before coding with Python, you need to set up your development environment.

Installation

Windows:

Visit the official Python website (https://www.python.org) and download the latest version of Python.

Run the installer and follow the installation prompts.

macOS:

Python is pre-installed on most macOS systems. You can also install it via package managers like Homebrew or download it from the official website.

Linux:

Python often comes pre-installed.

Use your distribution's package manager (e.g., apt for Ubuntu) to install Python.

Python Environments

Python offers various environments for writing and executing code:

IDLE (Integrated Development and Learning Environment):

A simple IDE included with Python.

Jupyter Notebooks:

Ideal for data analysis and visualization, providing an interactive environment.

Text Editors:

Use editors like VSCode, Sublime Text, or Atom, coupled with Python extensions, for a customized coding experience.

Our First Python Program

Let's write our first Python script, the traditional "Hello, World!" program, to ensure your setup is working:

```
print("Hello, World!")
```

To run this program:

Open a text editor or IDE.

Type the code above.

Save the file with a ".py" extension (e.g., hello.py).

Open a terminal or command prompt.

Navigate to the directory where your file is saved.

Type python hello.py and press Enter.

Congratulations! You've executed your first Python program.

Exploring Python Syntax

Python's syntax is clean and readable.

Some fundamental aspects include:

Indentation:

Python uses indentation to denote blocks of code, ensuring readability.

Comments:

single line comments:

Use # to add comments for better code understanding.

Multi line comments:

Type ''' or """ , just before the comment. And type ''' or """ immediately after the last line of comment

the purpose of comments is 2-fold

1. when you want to provide documentation in your program so that it is easily understandable later you will insert comments in your code.
2. When you want to hide certain "code components" in order to test other components, you can hide those code components by treating them as multi line comments

(comments are ignored by the compiler)

CHAPTER TWO

Python Fundamentals

Variables and Data Types:

Exploring different data types (integers, strings, lists, tuples, dictionaries, etc.) and variable assignments.

A Closer Look at Variables

First things first, let's understand the concept of variables in Python.

Variables are like containers that store information.

We'll learn how to create variables, assign values to them, and manipulate their contents.

We'll also learn how variables act as placeholders for various data types.

such as numbers, strings, or more complex objects. In Python, declaring a variable is straightforward; you just assign a value to it using the equal sign (=).

Example:

name = "Ashok" # Here, 'name' is a variable storing a string value 'Ashok'.

age = 64 # 'age' is a variable holding an integer value 25.

is_student = True # 'is_student' is a variable with a boolean value True.

Data Types in Python:

Python supports various data types that define the kind of values variables can hold. Some fundamental data types in Python include:

Integers (int):

Whole numbers without decimal points.

my_integer = 10

- **Floating-Point Numbers (float):** Numbers with decimal points.

my_float = 3.14

- **Strings (str):**

Ordered sequence of characters enclosed in quotes (single, double, or triple quotes).

my_string = 'Hello, Python!'

- **Booleans (bool):**

Represents True or False.

is_valid = True

- **Lists (list):**

Ordered collection of items enclosed in square brackets [].

my_list = [1, 2, 3, 4, 5]

- **Tuples (tuple):**

Ordered collection of items enclosed in parentheses ().

Unlike lists, tuples are immutable (cannot be modified, once they are assigned values).

my_tuple = (10, 20, 30)

- **Dictionaries (dict):**

Collection of key-value pairs enclosed in curly braces {}.

my_dict = {'name': 'John', 'age': 25, 'is_student': True}

Operators and Expressions

Arithmetic, comparison, logical, and assignment operators.

Arithmetic Operations:

addition = 5 + 3 # Addition

subtraction = 7 - 4 # Subtraction

multiplication = 2 * 6 # Multiplication

division = 10 / 2 # Division

String

concatenate = "Hello" + " " + "World!" # String Concatenation

Boolean Operations:

And operation = True and False # Logical AND

Or operation = True or False # Logical OR

Not operation = not True # Logical NOT

Control Flow:

In Python, loop control structures are used to execute a block of code repeatedly based on certain conditions. There are mainly two types of loops in Python:

for loops and while loops.

(Additionally, there are loop control statements like break, continue, and pass that help manage the flow within loops).

for loop:

The for loop in Python is used to iterate over a sequence (such as a list, tuple, string, or dictionary) or an iterable object.

Syntax:

for item in sequence:

code block to be executed

Here, item represents the current element in the sequence, and the loop iterates through each element until the sequence ends.

Example:

fruits = [‘apple’, ‘banana’, ‘cherry’] for fruit in fruits: print(fruit)

while loop:

The while loop in Python repeatedly executes a block of code as long as a specified condition is True.

Syntax:

```
while condition:
# code block to be executed
```

The loop continues until the condition becomes False.

Example:

```
num = 1
while num <= 5:
print(num)
num += 1
```

Output:

1 2 3 4 5

Loop Control Statements:

break, continue, and else

break Statement:

It terminates the loop prematurely based on a certain condition.

Example:

```
for i in range(1, 10):
if i == 5:
break
print(i)
```

Output:

1 2 3 4

continue Statement:

It skips the current iteration and continues zto the next iteration of the loop.

Example:

```
for i in range(1, 6):
if i == 3:
continue
print(i)
```

pass Statement:

It is a null operation that does nothing. It is used when a statement is required syntactically but you want to skip execution.

Example:

```
for i in range(1, 4):
pass # do nothing
```

These loop control statements provide ways to manipulate the flow of the loop execution, allowing for more flexibility in handling iterations within the loop structures in Python.

Conditional statements:

Conditional statements steer our code based on different conditions.

et us dive into the world of if, elif, and else statements, learning how Python makes decisions and executes code paths accordingly.

if statements:

Syntax:

```
if condition:
# Code block if condition is True
```

Example:

```
x = 10
if x > 5:
print("x is greater than 5")
```

Output

```
x is greater than 5
```

if-else Statements:

Syntax:

```
if condition:
# Code block if condition is True
els Example:
ondition1 is True
elif condition2:
```

```
# Code block if condition2 is True
else:
# Code block if none of the above conditions are True
```

Example:

```
z = 7
if z < 0:
print("z is negative")
elif z == 0:
print("z is zero")
else:
print("z is positive")
```

Output:

z is positive

else in loops:

```
for i in range(5):
print(i)
else:
print("Loop completed without a break")
```

Enhanced for Loop

Syntax:

```
for item in iterable:
# Code block to execute for each item in the) iterable
fruits=[“apple", "banana", "orange"]
for fruit in fruits:
print(fruit)
```

Output:

Appleb

banana

orange

Control statements help in controlling the flow of execution based on conditions and iterating through sequences of data. These constructs are powerful tools in Python for decision-making and repetitive tasks.

CHAPTER THREE

Functions and Modules

Functions in Python:

A function in Python is a block of reusable code that performs a specific task. Functions help in organizing and modularizing code, making it more readable and maintainable.

The basic structure of a function:

```
def function_name(parameters):
# Code block
# Perform some tasks
return result
```

def

This keyword is used to define a function.

This is the name of the function. One should choose a descriptive name that reflects the function's purpose.

parameters:

These are variables that you can pass to the function. They are optional, depending on the function's requirements.

Code block:

The indented block of code under the function definition is the body of the function. It contains the instructions to execute when the function is called.

return:

This keyword is used to return a value from the function. It is optional; if omitted, the function returns None.

Here's an example:

```
def add_numbers(a, b):
result = a + b
return result
sum_result = add_numbers(3, 5)
print(sum_result) # Output: 8
```

Modules in Python:

A module in Python is a file containing Python definitions and statements. These files can be reused in other Python scripts by importing them. A module can contain functions, classes, and variables. Here's a simple example of a module:

Example module: math_operations.py

```
def add(a, b):
return a + b
def subtract(a, b):
return a – b
```

You can use this module in another script like this:

```
# Using the module in another script
import math_operations
result_add = math_operations.add(10, 5)
result_subtract = math_operations.subtract(10, 5)
print(result_add) # Output: 15
print(result_subtract) # Output: 5
```

In this example, math_operations is a module, and add and subtract are functions defined within that module.

Functions allow you to encapsulate and reuse code, while modules provide a way to organize and reuse collections of related functions, classes, and variables.

Built-in Functions and Libraries:

Functions and Libraries:

ChatGPT

In Python, built-in functions and libraries play a crucial role in simplifying and enhancing the development process. Let me provide you with an overview and some code examples:

Built-in Functions

len()

Returns the length (the number of items) of an object.

```
my_list = [1, 2, 3, 4, 5]
length_of_list = len(my_list)
print(length_of_list) # Output: 5
```

max() and min():

Returns the maximum and minimum values of a sequence or arguments.

```
numbers = [10, 5, 8, 20, 15]
max_value = max(numbers)
min_value = min(numbers)
print(max_value, min_value) # Output: 20 5
```

sum()

Returns the sum of all items in a sequence.

```
numbers = [1, 2, 3, 4, 5]
sum_of_numbers = sum(numbers)
print(sum_of_numbers) # Output: 15
```

sorted()

Returns a new sorted list from the elements of any iterable.

```
unsorted_list = [3, 1, 4, 1, 5, 9, 2, 6, 5]
sorted_list = sorted(unsorted_list)
print(sorted_list) # Output: [1, 1, 2, 3, 4, 5, 5, 6, 9]
```

Libraries:

math Library

Provides mathematical functions.

```
import math
sqrt_value = math.sqrt(25)
print(sqrt_value) # Output: 5.0
```

random Library:

Used for generating random numbers.

```
import random
random_number = random.randint(1, 10)
print(random_number)
```

datetime Library:

Provides classes for working with dates and times.

```
from datetime import datetime
current_time = datetime.now()
print(current_time)
```

These examples provide just a glimpse of the vast array of built-in functions and libraries available in Python. They offer powerful tools for developers to efficiently perform common tasks and extend functionality in their programs.Python has ap extensive

CHAPTER FOUR

Data Structures and Collections

Lists and Tuples:

Understanding mutable and immutable sequences and their operations.

Lists:

A list is an ordered, mutable collection of elements. Lists are versatile and can contain elements of different data types. You can modify the contents of a list by adding, removing, or changing elements. Lists are defined using square brackets [].

Example:

Creating a list

my_list = [1, 2, 'hello', 3.14, True] #

Accessing elements print(my_list[0])

Output: 1

print(my_list[2])

Output: 'hello'

Modifying elements my_list[1] = 'world'

print(my_list) #

Output: [1, 'world', 'hello', 3.14, True]

Appending elements

my_list.append(42)

```
print(my_list)
# Output: [1, 'world', 'hello', 3.14, True, 42]
# Removing elements by value
my_list.remove('hello')
print(my_list)
# Output: [1, 'world', 3.14, True, 42]
# Removing elements by index
removed_element = my_list.pop(2)
print(removed_element)
# Output: 3.14 print(my_list)
# Output: [1, 'world', True, 42]
# Slicing
subset = my_list[1:3]
print(subset)
# Output: ['world', True]
# Iterating through elements for item in my_list:
print(item) # Output: # 1 # world # True # 42
```

In the example above, my_list is a list containing a mix of integers, strings, a float, and a boolean. You can modify the list by changing values, appending new elements, or removing existing ones. The ability to modify lists makes them useful for dynamic collections of data in various programming scenarios.

Tuples:

A tuple is an ordered, immutable collection of elements. Once a tuple is created, you cannot modify its contents (immutable). However, you can access elements using indexing. Tuples are defined using parentheses ().

Example:

```
# Creating a tuple
my_tuple = (1, 2, 'hello', 3.14, True)
# Accessing elements print(my_tuple[0])
# Output: 1
```

```
print(my_tuple[2])
# Output: 'hello'
# Tuple unpacking
a, b, c, d, e = my_tuple print(a, b, c, d, e)
# Output:
1 2 'hello' 3.14 True
```

In the example above, my_tuple contains a mix of integers, strings, a float, and a boolean. Tuples are useful when you want to group related pieces of data together, and their immutability ensures that the data remains constant throughout the program.

Returning Multiple Values from Functions:

Tuples are often used to return multiple values from a function.

```
def get_coordinates():
return (10, 20)
x, y = get_coordinates()
print("X:", x, "Y:", y)
# Output: X: 10 Y: 20
```

Immutable Data:

If you have a set of values that should not be modified, using a tuple is a good choice.

```
dimensions = (800, 600)
```

Dictionary Keys:

Tuples can be used as keys in dictionaries, which is not possible with lists because lists are mutable.

```
coordinates_dict = {('A', 1): 'Point A', ('B', 2): 'Point B'}
```

Data Integrity:

The immutability of tuples ensures data integrity in situations where you want to prevent accidental modification of values.

Note:

While tuples are immutable, the elements they contain may be mutable. For example, if a tuple contains a list, you can modify the list inside the tuple. However, you cannot reassign a new value to an existing position in the tuple.

Dictionaries:

Exploring key-value pairs and dictionary manipulation.

Dictionaries:

A dictionary is an unordered collection of key-value pairs. Each key must be unique, and the values can be of any data type. Dictionaries are defined using curly braces {}.

Example:

```
# Creating a dictionary
my_dict = {'name': 'John', 'age': 25, 'city': 'New York'}
# Accessing values by key print(my_dict['name'])
# Output:
'John' print(my_dict['age'])
# Output:
25
# Modifying values
my_dict['age'] = 26
print(my_dict['age'])
# Output:
26 # Adding a new key-value pair
my_dict['occupation'] = 'Engineer'
print(my_dict['occupation'])
# Output: 'Engineer'
# Checking if a key exists
if 'city' in my_dict:
print("City:", my_dict['city'])
# Output:4
'New York'
# Iterating through key-value pairs:
```

for key, value in my_dict.items():
print(key, ":", value)
# Output:
# name : John # age : 26 # city : New York # occupation : Engineer

In the example above, my_dict is a dictionary with keys ('name', 'age', 'city') and their corresponding values. The keys provide a way to access the associated values efficiently.

Use Cases:

Storing Key-Value Pairs:

Dictionaries are excellent for storing information that can be represented as key-value pairs.

student_grades = {'Alice': 90, 'Bob': 85, 'Charlie': 92}

Fast Data Retrieval:

Retrieving a value from a dictionary by its key is very fast, making dictionaries suitable for scenarios where efficient data lookup is required.

Configuration Settings:

Dictionaries are commonly used to store configuration settings for applications.

config = {'debug_mode': True, 'max_connections': 100}

Dynamic Data Structures:

Dictionaries allow dynamic addition and removal of key-value pairs, making them flexible for handling changing data.

user_info = {'username': 'john_doe', 'password': 'secure123'} user_info['email'] = 'john@example.com'

JSON-like Structures:

Dictionaries are often used to represent data in a format similar to JSON.

person_data = {'name': 'Alice', 'age': 30, 'address': {'city': 'Wonderland', 'zip': '12345'}}

Dictionaries are a fundamental part of Python, providing a convenient and efficient way to organize and manipulate data.

CHAPTER FIVE

Chapter 5: Object-Oriented Programming (OOP)

Object-oriented programming is a programming paradigm that revolves around the concept of objects, which can contain data in the form of attributes (variables) and behavior in the form of methods (functions).

In Python, everything is an object. Classes are used to create theseobjects, providing a blueprint for their structure and behavior. Let's explore some key concepts in OOP using Python:

Classes and Objects:

A class is a blueprint that defines the properties (attributes) and behaviors (methods) that objects of the class will have. To create an instance of a class (i.e., an object), you use the class as a template.

Example:

```
class Car:
def __init__(self, make, model):
self.make = make
self.model = model
```

```
def display_info(self):
print(f"This is a {self.make} {self.model}")
# Creating an instance of the Car class
my_car = Car("Toyota", "Corolla")
my_car.display_info()
# Output: This is a Toyota Corolla
```

Attributes and Methods

Attributes are variables that hold data within a class, while methods are functions defined within a class to perform operations on the object's data.

Example:

```
class Circle:
def __init__(self, radius):
self.radius = radius
def area(self):
return 3.14159 * self.radius ** 2
def circumference(self):
return 2 * 3.14159 * self.radius
```

Creating an instance of the Circle class

```
my_circle = Circle(5)
print(my_circle.area())
# Output: 78.53975
print(my_circle.circumference())
# Output: 31.4159
```

Inheritance:

Inheritance allows a new class (subclass) to inherit attributes and methods from an existing class (superclass). This promotes code reusability and the creation of a hierarchy of classes.

Example:

```
class Animal:
def make_sound(self):
pass
```

```
class Dog(Animal):
def make_sound(self):
print("Woof!")
class Cat(Animal):
def make_sound(self):
print("Meow!")
my_dog = Dog()
my_dog.make_sound() # Output: Woof!
my_cat = Cat()
my_cat.make_sound() # Output: Meow!
```

Encapsulation, Abstraction, Inheritance, Polymorphism:

Encapsulation

The bundling of data with the methods that operate on that data, restricting direct access to some of the object's components.

Abstraction

Hiding complex implementation details and showing only the necessary features of an object.

Polymorphism:

The ability to present the same interface for different data types or objects.

These concepts further enhance the flexibility and maintainability of your code by promoting modularity and reducing complexity.

Understanding how to create classes and objects in Python is fundamental for utilizing the power of object-oriented programming, enabling code organization, reusability, and abstraction.Implementing classes, +constructors, methods, and attributes.

Advanced OOP Concepts:

Advanced Object-Oriented Programming (OOP) concepts in Python extend beyond the basics of classes and objects. They include inheritance, polymorphism, encapsulation, abstraction, and more. Let's dive into these concepts:

Inheritance:

Inheritance is a powerful feature in OOP that allows a new class (subclass) to inherit properties (attributes and methods) from an existing class (superclass). It promotes code reuse and enables the creation of a hierarchy of classes.

Example:

```
class Animal:
def sound(self):
pass
class Dog(Animal):
def sound(self):
return "Woof!"
class Cat(Animal):
def sound(self):
return "Meow!"
```

Animal is the superclass, and Dog and Cat are subclasses inheriting from Animal.

Subclasses can override methods from the superclass, as seen in the sound() method.

Polymorphism:

Polymorphism allows objects of different classes to be treated as objects of a common superclass. It involves using a single interface to represent different data types or objects.

Example:

```
def animal_sound(animal):
return animal.sound()
dog = Dog()
cat = Cat()
```

```
print(animal_sound(dog)) # Output: "Woof!"
print(animal_sound(cat)) # Output: "Meow!"
```

The animal_sound() function takes an object of the Animal superclass as an argument and calls the sound() method.

Both Dog and Cat objects can be passed to animal_sound(), demonstrating polymorphic behavior.

3. Encapsulation:

Encapsulation refers to bundling data (attributes) and methods that operate on that data within a class, limiting access to the inner workings of an object and preventing direct modification of its state.

Example:

```
class BankAccount:
def __init__(self):
self._balance = 0 # Private attribute
def deposit(self, amount):
self._balance += amount
def get_balance(self):
return self._balance
```

_balance is marked as a private attribute (conventionally, not enforced) using a single underscore, indicating that it shouldn't be accessed directly from outside the class.

4. Abstraction

Abstraction hides complex implementation details and exposes only the necessary features of an object. It allows focusing on essential functionalities while hiding unnecessary details.

Example:

```
from abc import ABC, abstractmethod
class Shape(ABC):
@abstractmethod
```

```
def area(self):
pass
class Circle(Shape):
def __init__(self, radius):
self.radius = radius
def area(self):
return 3.14159 * self.radius ** 2
```

Shape is an abstract class with an abstract method area() that needs to be implemented by its subclasses.

Circle inherits from Shape and implements the area() method.

These advanced OOP concepts in Python enhance code modularity, reusability, and maintainability, allowing for better organization and scalability of complex programs.

CHAPTER SIX

File Handling and Input/Output Operations

Reading and Writing Files:

Opening a File:

Use the open() function to open a file in different modes (read, write, append).

```
# Open a file in read mode
file_path = 'example.txt'
with open(file_path, 'r') as file:
# File operations go here
```

Reading Entire File Content:

Use the read() method to read the entire content of the file.

```
Python
with open(file_path, 'r') as file:
content = file.read()
print(content)
```

Reading Line by Line:

Use a loop to read the file line by line using the readline() method.

with open(file_path, 'r') as file:
for line in file:
print(line.strip()) # strip() removes extra newline characters.

Reading into a List:

Use the readlines() method to read all lines into a list.

with open(file_path, 'r') as file:
lines = file.readlines()
for line in lines:
print(line.strip())

Writing Files:

Opening a File for Writing:

Use the open() function with the 'w' mode to open a file for writing. If the file doesn't exist, it will be created. Be cautious, as this will overwrite existing content.

with open('new_file.txt', 'w') as file:
File operations go here

Writing Content:

Use the write() method to write content to the file.

with open('new_file.txt', 'w') as file:
file.write('Hello, this is a new file!')

Appending to a File:

Use the 'a' mode in open() to open a file for appending.

with open('existing_file.txt', 'a') as file:
file.write('This line will be appended.\n')

Handling Exceptions:

Always use file operations within a try block and handle exceptions using except blocks.

python
try:
with open('example.txt', 'r') as file:
content = file.read()

```
print(content)
except FileNotFoundError:
print("File not found!")
except Exception as e:
print(f"An error occurred: {e}")
```

Closing Files:

Using the with statement automatically closes the file when the block is exited. However, if you open a file without with, remember to explicitly close it using close().

```
file = open('example.txt', 'r')
content = file.read()
file.close()
```

Using Context Managers:

The with statement is a context manager that ensures proper resource management. It's a recommended practice for file handling.

Example:

```
try:
with open('example.txt', 'r') as file:
content = file.read()
print(content)
except FileNotFoundError:
print("File not found!")
except Exception as e:
print(f"An error occurred: {e}")
with open('new_file.txt', 'w') as file:
file.write('Hello, this is a new file!')
with open('existing_file.txt', 'a') as file:
file.write('This line will be appended.\n')
```

CHAPTER SEVEN

Advanced Topics in Python

Regular Expressions:

Regular expressions (regex or regexp) in Python are a powerful tool for pattern matching and text manipulation. The re module in Python provides support for regular expressions. Here's a brief explanation of key concepts and functionalities:

Importing the re Module:

To use regular expressions in Python, you need to import the re module.

```
import re
```

Basic Patterns:

Regular expressions consist of special characters that form patterns. For example:

.: Matches any character except a newline.

^: Anchors the pattern at the start of the string.

$: Anchors the pattern at the end of the string.

Character Classes:

[ ]: Defines a character class. For example, [aeiou] matches any vowel.

[^]: Negates a character class. For example, [^0-9] matches any non-digit.

Quantifiers:

*: Matches 0 or more occurrences of the preceding character.

+: Matches 1 or more occurrences of the preceding character.

?: Matches 0 or 1 occurrence of the preceding character.

{m}: Matches exactly m occurrences.

{m, n}: Matches between m and n occurrences.

Special Characters:

\: Escapes a special character, allowing you to match it as a literal (e.g., \\ matches a backslash).

|: Acts like an OR operator, allowing you to match either of two patterns.

Grouping and Capturing:

(): Groups patterns together. Also used for capturing sub-patterns.

(?:): Non-capturing group.

Anchors:

\b: Word boundary.

\B: Not a word boundary.

^ (caret): Anchors the pattern at the beginning of a line.

$: Anchors the pattern at the end of a line.

Common Functions in re Module:

re.search(pattern, string): Searches the string for a match.

re.match(pattern, string):

Checks if the pattern occurs at the start of the string.

re.findall(pattern, string):

Returns a list of all matches in the string.

re.sub(pattern, replacement, string):

Replaces occurrences of the pattern with the replacement.

Here's a simple example that uses regular expressions to find email addresses in a given text:

```
import re
text = "Contact us at support@example.com or info@example.org for assistance."
email_pattern = r‘\b[A-Za-z0-9._%+-]+@[A-Za-z0-9.-]+\.[A-Z|a-z]{2,}\b’
emails = re.findall(email_pattern, text)
print(emails)
```

This example demonstrates a basic use of regular expressions to extract email addresses from a text. Regular expressions are highly versatile and can be applied invarious scenarios for efficient text processing in Python.

Concurrency and Parallelism:

Concurrency and parallelism are two concepts in the realm of computing, particularly in Python, that deal with the execution of multiple tasks.

Concurrency:

Concurrency refers to the ability of a system to handle multiple tasks seemingly simultaneously. In a concurrent system, tasks are executed independently, and the execution order may not necessarily follow a strict sequence. In Python, concurrency is often achieved through techniques such as multi-threading and asynchronous programming.

Multi-threading:

Python's threading module allows developers to create and manage multiple threads within a single process. Each thread runs independently, sharing the same resources, but it provides the illusion of simultaneous execution.

Asynchronous Programming:

Python 3.5 and above introduced the asyncio module, which enables asynchronous programming using the async/await syntax. This allows non-blocking execution of tasks, enabling the program to perform other tasks while waiting for I/O operations to complete.

Parallelism:

Parallelism, on the other hand, involves the simultaneous execution of multiple tasks to improve performance and reduce execution time. In parallel computing, tasks are broken down into smaller sub-tasks that are executed concurrently on separate processors or cores. Python supports parallelism through various approaches:

Multiprocessing:

The multiprocessing module in Python allows for the creation of separate processes, each with its own interpreter and memory space. This enables true parallelism as each process runs independently, utilizing multiple CPU cores.

Parallel Processing Libraries: Python also has libraries like concurrent.futures and joblib that provide high-level interfaces for parallel processing. These libraries simplify the creation and management of parallel tasks.

Key Differences:

1. Concurrency is about dealing with many tasks at the same time, but not necessarily simultaneously. Parallelism is about executing many tasks simultaneously.

1. Concurrency is achieved through techniques like multi-threading and asynchronous programming. Parallelism is achieved through multiple processes or threads

running in parallel.

Concurrency is more focused on the structure of the program, while parallelism is more focused on performance improvement.

In Python, the Global Interpreter Lock (GIL) has implications for both concurrency and parallelism. The GIL allows only one thread to execute Python bytecode at a time, limiting the effectiveness of multi-threading for CPU-bound tasks. However, for I/O-bound tasks, concurrency and asynchronous programming can still be beneficial.

It's essential to choose the right approach (concurrency or parallelism) based on the nature of your tasks and the specific requirements of your Python application.Exploring multithreading and multiprocessing concepts.

GUI Programming:

GUI (Graphical User Interface) programming in Python involves creating visual interfaces for users to interact with applications. Python provides several libraries for GUI development, each with its own set of features and use cases. Two popular GUI libraries in Python are Tkinter and PyQt.

Tkinter:

Tkinter is the standard GUI toolkit that comes with Python. It provides a simple way to create windows, dialogs, buttons, and other GUI elements.

Creating a Simple Window:

```
import tkinter as tk
root = tk.Tk()
root.title("My GUI App")
label = tk.Label(root, text="Hello, Tkinter!")
label.pack()
root.mainloop()
```

Widgets:

Tkinter offers various widgets like Label, Button, Entry, etc., that you can use to build your GUI.

Layout Management:

Tkinter provides geometry managers (pack, grid, and place) to organize and arrange widgets in the GUI.

PyQt:

PyQt is a set of Python bindings for Qt, a popular C++ GUI framework. It offers more advanced features and is suitable for larger and more complex applications.

Installation:

```
pip install PyQt5
```

Creating a Simple Window:

```
from PyQt5.QtWidgets import QApplication, QLabel, QWidget
app = QApplication([])
window = QWidget()
window.setWindowTitle("My GUI App")
label = QLabel("Hello, PyQt!")
label.show()
app.exec_()
```

Signal and Slot Mechanism:

PyQt uses a signal and slot mechanism for event handling, allowing you to connect events to functions.

Qt Designer:

PyQt includes Qt Designer, a visual design tool that enables you to design your GUI by dragging and dropping components.

Kivy:

Kivy is another Python GUI framework that is particularly useful for developing multi-touch applications. It is cross-platform and supports both desktop and mobile development.

Installation:

```
pip install kivy
```

Creating a Simple Window:

```
from kivy.app import App
from kivy.uix.label import Label
class MyApp(App):
def build(self):
return Label(text='Hello, Kivy!')
if __name__ == '__main__':
MyApp().run()
```

Touch Events:

Kivy is designed with touch interfaces in mind, making it suitable for mobile app development.

These are just a few examples, and the choice of a GUI library depends on the specific requirements of your application. Whether you opt for Tkinter, PyQt, Kivy, or other libraries, Python provides powerful tools for creating visually appealing and interactive graphical user interfaces.

Introduction to graphical user interface development using libraries like Tkinter or PyQt.

www.ingramcontent.com/pod-product-compliance
Lightning Source LLC
LaVergne TN
LVHW021202160826
845679LV00024B/2218